POOH'S LITTLE
INSTRUCTION BOOK

INSPIRED BY
A. A. Milne

POOH'S LITTLE
INSTRUCTION BOOK

WITH DECORATIONS BY
Ernest H. Shepard

METHUEN

First published in Great Britain in 1996 by Methuen
an imprint of Reed Books, Children's Publishing
Michelin House, 81 Fulham Road, London SW3 6RB
and Auckland, Melbourne, Singapore and Toronto
First published as a paperback by Methuen in 1995
Published in the United States 1995 by Dutton Children's Books
Copyright © 1995 by the Trustees of the Pooh Properties
Text by A.A. Milne and illustrations by E.H. Shepard
from *Winnie-the-Pooh* and *The House at Pooh Corner*
Copyright under the Berne Convention
This presentation copyright © Dutton Children's Books
a division of Penguin Books USA Inc.
Written by Joan Powers Designed by Joseph Rutt
3 5 7 9 10 8 6 4

Produced by Mandarin Offset
Printed and bound in China

ISBN 0 416 19375 7

🐾 If possible, try to find a way to come downstairs that doesn't involve going bump, bump, bump, on the back of your head.

🐾 When speaking to a Bear of Very Little Brain, remember that long words may Bother him.

🐝 When carrying a jar of honey to give to a friend for his birthday, don't stop and eat it along the way.

🐝 Don't forget that a tail is a tail; it isn't just a Little Bit Extra at the back.

♣ It is more fun to talk with someone who doesn't use long, difficult words but rather short, easy words like "What about lunch?"

♣ When you see someone putting on his Big Boots, you can be pretty sure that an Adventure is going to happen.

▪ Despite their claims to the contrary, Tiggers don't really like everything.

▪ Drinking your milk and talking at the same time may result in your having to be patted on the back and dried for quite a long time afterwards.

"They're funny things, Accidents.
You never have them till you're
having them."

—*Eeyore*

🐾 Rivers know this: There is no hurry. We shall get there some day.

🐾 Keep in mind that, at least to Eeyore, the letter A represents Learning, Education, and all the things Pooh and Piglet haven't got.

🐾 A little Consideration, a little Thought for Others, makes all the difference.

🐾 Always watch where you are going. Otherwise, you may step on a piece of the Forest that was left out by mistake.

❦ Not everyone appreciates being hooshed to the bank of the river by having a large stone dropped on them.

❦ Never go indoors to practise a special Outdoor Song which Has To Be Sung In The Snow.

Try not to sit down on thistles; it takes all of the Life out of them. Besides, someone might have planned on eating them for lunch.

- When looking at your two paws, as soon as you have decided which of them is the right one, then you can be sure the other one is the left.

- The trick to succeeding at Poohsticks is letting your stick drop in a twitchy sort of way.

&. To the uneducated, an A is just three sticks.

&. If you secretly get into a kangaroo's pocket and she begins to jump away, be prepared for a bumpy ride.

"You can't help respecting anybody who can spell Tuesday, even if he doesn't spell it right."

—*Rabbit*

&. The best place to dig a Very Deep Pit in which to catch a Heffalump is somewhere where a Heffalump is, only about a foot farther on.

&. When having a smackerel of something with a friend, don't eat so much that you get stuck in the doorway trying to get out.

❖ A Proper Tea is much nicer than a Very Nearly Tea, which is one you forget about afterwards.

❖ When late morning rolls around and you're feeling a bit out of sorts, don't worry; you're probably just a little eleven o'clockish.

When you're visiting a friend and you find that it is time for a little smackerel of something, try looking wistfully in the direction of the cupboard.

"It's always useful to know where a friend-and-relation *is*, whether you want him or whether you don't."

—*Rabbit*

Just because an animal is large, it doesn't mean
he doesn't want kindness; however big Tigger
seems to be, remember that he wants as much
kindness as Roo.

When you are a Bear of Very Little Brain, and you Think of Things, you find sometimes that a Thing which seemed very Thingish inside you is quite different when it gets out into the open and has other people looking at it.

⚘ If you plant a haycorn, it will grow up into an oak-tree. But it doesn't follow that if you plant a honeycomb, it will grow up into a beehive.

🐝 Be especially careful in dangerous places where an Ambush might occur. An Ambush is a sort of Surprise. Then again, so is a gorse-bush sometimes.

♣ When setting off on an Expotition, be sure to bring Provisions. Or, at the very least, things to eat.

☩ When going round a spinney of larch trees Tracking Something, be sure it isn't your own footprints you are following.

♨ Being fine today doesn't Mean Anything.
It may hail a good deal tomorrow—blizzards
and whatnot.

"We can't all, and some of us don't.
That's all there is to it."

—*Eeyore*

🐜 When conversing with Owls, remember that they think it is rather beneath them to talk about little cake things with pink sugar icing.

"When you go after honey with a balloon, the great thing is not to let the bees know you're coming."

—*Winnie-the-Pooh*

❀ Before floating up into the sky with a balloon in search of honey, make sure the bees you are looking for are the right sort of bees.

❀ Something about the way Very Bouncy Animals say How-do-you-do tends to leave one's ears full of sand.

❁ People who don't Think probably don't have Brains; rather, they have grey fluff that's blown into their heads by mistake.

🐾 When trying to catch a Heffalump, remember that the trap you set must be a Cunning Trap.

🐾 When waking in the morning, remember that whether your first thought is "What's for breakfast?" or "I wonder what's going to happen exciting *today*?" it's the same thing.

🐝 When you've been walking in the wind for miles, and you suddenly go into somebody's house, and he says, "You're just in time for a little smackerel of something," then it's a Friendly Day.

"Brains first and then Hard Work."

—*Eeyore*

♭ When checking your Heffalump Trap for Heffalumps, be sure to bring along a piece of string to lead them home with.

♭ When selecting a new bell-rope for your front door, make sure it isn't someone else's tail.

🐝 When you are pretty sure that an Adventure is going to happen, brush the honey off your nose and spruce yourself up as best you can, so as to look Ready for Anything.

"Nobody can be un-cheered with a balloon."

—*Winnie-the-Pooh*

🐾 When you come across Eeyore in the Forest and he seems even gloomier than usual, check to see if he has his tail. It may be missing.

🐾 When trying to ignore a knock at your door, don't yell out, "No!" when someone asks, "Is anybody at home?"

🐾 When in doubt, keep in mind that "O gallant
Piglet" is always a very thoughtful way of
beginning a piece of poetry.

❦ It isn't much good having anything exciting like floods, if you can't share them with somebody.

❦ If the person you are talking to doesn't appear to be listening, be patient. It may simply be that he has a small piece of fluff in his ear.

When climbing up a tree on the back of a Tigger, be sure to find out before you start if the Tigger knows how to climb down.

🐝 When someone you love is wedged in a
   doorway and must wait to get thin enough
   to get out, read him a Sustaining Book, such
   as would help and comfort him.

🐝 If you want to make a song more hummy, add
   a few *tiddely poms*.

🐝 When searching for someone, it's a good idea
to determine whether the missing person is the
sort of friend-and-relation who settles on one's
nose, or the sort who might get trodden on
by mistake.

"It is hard to be brave, when you're only a Very Small Animal."

—*Piglet*

- You can't stay in your corner of the Forest waiting for others to come to you. You have to go to them sometimes.

- When your house looks like a tree that has blown down, it is time to get a new house.

☙ When you fall on somebody, it's not enough to say you didn't mean to; after all, he probably didn't mean to be underneath you.

☙ If you look round and see a Very Fierce Heffalump looking down at you, sometimes you forget what you were going to say.

&. If someone asks you how a new resident came to be there, and you don't know, just say, "In the Usual Way, if you know what I mean."

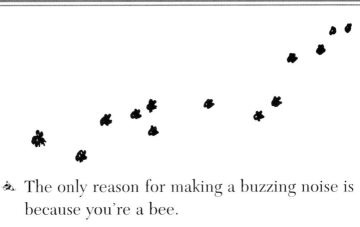

🐝 The only reason for making a buzzing noise is because you're a bee.

🐝 Before beginning a Hunt, it is wise to ask someone what you are looking for before you begin looking for it.

"Sometimes, when people have quite finished taking a person's house, there are one or two bits which they don't want and are rather glad for the person to take back."

—*Eeyore*

❦ If you've eaten the honey that was meant as a
   birthday gift for a friend, just wash out the pot,
   get somebody to write "A Happy Birthday" on
   it, and present the pot as a gift.

❦ It gets you nowhere if the other person's tail
   is only just in sight for the second half of the
   conversation.

🐾 Sometimes a boat is a boat, and sometimes it's more of an Accident. It depends on whether you're on top of it or underneath it.

If you are looking for Home and find instead a sand-pit, try looking for a sand-pit. Then you'd be sure not to find it, which would be a Good Thing, because you might find something that you *weren't* looking for, which might be just what you *were* looking for.

♣ A Very Clever Brain can catch a Heffalump,
   if only he knows the right way to go about it.

♣ Even though eating honey is a very good thing
   to do, there is a moment just before you begin
   to eat it which is better.

🐝 Always be aware of how many pots of honey you have in the cupboard; it's nice to be able to say, "I've got fourteen pots of honey left." Or fifteen, as the case may be.

❦ Drop in on anyone, at any time, if you feel like it. If they say "Bother," you can drop out again.

❦ Those who are clever, who have Brain, never understand anything.

❧ Sometimes, if you stand on the bottom rail of a bridge and lean over to watch the river slipping slowly away beneath you, you will suddenly know everything there is to be known.

❧ In case of Sudden and Temporary Immersion, the Important Thing is to keep the Head Above Water.

❦ Tiggers can climb trees. Of course, there's the coming-down, too, which is difficult, unless one falls, in which case it is . . . easy.

❦ A bear, however hard he tries,
Grows tubby without exercise.

"Poetry and Hums aren't things which you get, they're things which get *you*. And all you can do is to go where they can find you."

—*Winnie-the-Pooh*

🐾 When someone gives you a bath that you really don't want, one which changes your colour, remember that you can roll in the dirt on the way home to get your nice comfortable colour again.

🐾 If you're standing on the slippery bank of a river, be careful. If somebody bounces you loudly from behind, you'll probably slip.

🐾 If you think you see a Heffalump in a trap, make sure it isn't really a Bear with an empty jar of honey stuck on his head.

🐾 If you are trying to find your way home, and keep finding yourself instead back at the same sand-pit, it may be that the sand-pit is following you about.

"Spelling isn't everything. There are days when spelling Tuesday simply doesn't count."

—*Rabbit*

🐾 When making an expotition to discover the
   North Pole, be sure someone in the group
   knows what the North Pole looks like.
   (It's sure to be a pole stuck in the ground.)

"It's so much more friendly with two."

—*Piglet*

🐾 Don't underestimate the value of Doing
   Nothing, of just going along, listening to all
   the things you can't hear, and not bothering.